D0660721

PRAY HERS 31-DAY CHALLENGE

IN HERS IS YOURS

TAMARA L. DEAN

Copyright © 2014 Tamara L. Dean

First edition

All rights reserved. No part of this document may be reproduced or transmitted in any form or by any means, electronic, mechanical, photocopying, recording, or otherwise, without prior written permission of the publisher.

ISBN: 9780991411009

Library of Congress Control Number: 2014905505

Order at http://www.prayhers.com/ or:

Pray Hers
P.O. Box 203043
Arlington, TX 76006

Unless otherwise indicated, all Scripture quotations are taken from the King James Version (KJV) of the Holy Bible.

Scripture quotations marked NIV are from New International Version.

Scripture quotations marked MSG are taken from The Message Bible.

For every woman with a dream in her heart...
I pray yours.

CONTENTS

INTRODUCTION

The moment I woke up and my feet hit the floor, it was as if I had entered the devil's boxing ring unprepared. He swung and hit me with feelings of uncertainty concerning my purpose in life. He came at me with hopelessness and discouragement. Then with a left hook, I was panged with failure and disappointment over the lack of progression in my life. I felt behind in what I thought I needed to accomplish. The devil's goal was obvious—to knock me into a deep hole of self-pity. Needless to say, I felt defeated and forsaken.

I tried to call a friend for a little encouragement, but it seemed like every time I reached for the phone, the devil yanked it out of my hand. He convinced me that she was too busy and had her own problems to deal with. So there I was, alone in the ring with my tormentor, as he continued to jab away at my emotions.

Fortunately, that was the same day I was to attend a party where some faith-filled, devil-fighting, and praying women would also be in attendance. At the party, I pretended to have a good time. I laughed and talked, but in reality I was still in the ring with the devil and he was wearing me down mentally and emotionally. Finally, after spending hours fighting alone, I boldly interrupted the women as they were talking. I explained to them what I was contending with and asked them to pray for me. It was time to take control of the fight!

Four powerful women immediately jumped into the ring with me, surrounded me in a circle—as if to protect me—and began to battle in prayer. The intensity, unity, and power in their prayer were so tremendous; it knocked the devil dead on his face. I sensed an instant relief that was undeniable. It was at that moment I realized the power that is made available when women can come together with one accord. When women are not afraid of helping each other, good things happen, problems go away, and prayers are answered.

I wonder how many women have lost their fight to the devil only because there was no one around to jump in the ring with them and help them fight. How many times have you ignored the prompting to call a sister only to find out later, that was the day she needed you the most? I realize how busy life can be. I know how easy it is to become consumed with the demands of your own life, forgetting about others. But I have also come to realize the power that is made available when you take time to step outside of yourself in support of another person.

In Hers is Yours. What does that mean?

Imagine that you have an apple seed in your hand and you desire to have apples. Inside of the seed you are holding are the apples you desire, but the only way to get to the apples is to plant the seed into the ground.

You represent the apple seed. Your sister represents the ground. When you sow into HER life and the lives of others, you reap a return. The life of Jesus Christ is the greatest example of how sowing and reaping works. He walked the earth, giving unselfishly of Himself. He sowed kindness into the lives of people who were deemed unlovable. He ultimately sowed His entire body for the redemption of everyone and He is still reaping His return today.

Your return for sowing yourself into the lives of others will be immeasurable. You may never know how far and wide the fruit of your seed will spread. Do you want love? Sow love. Do you want finances? Sow finances. Do you want a husband? Pray for someone else to be blessed with a husband. Owning a seed will produce nothing, but sowing a seed will produce enough for everyone to partake.

Note: You may not necessarily receive from the person you are sowing into. Your harvest may come from elsewhere, but it will come. *"Be not deceived; God is not mocked: for whatsoever a man soweth, that shall he also reap" (Galatians 6:7).*

Why Take The PrayHers 31-Day Challenge?

I believe that we are in a season where God is going to use women more mightily than in times past. But for that to happen, we must rid ourselves of envy, backbiting, pride, people-pleasing tendencies, and needless competition. It's time to celebrate our uniqueness and unite our commonalities so that we can be more powerful in our existence.

Christ did it for us so let's do it for each other. Show forth God's love. In the end, you will sense God at work in your life and in the lives of those you have been praying for. For the next 31 days, as you open this book and pray on behalf of another person, you are sowing a powerful seed—you.

This is a challenge and challenges are not made to be easy or convenient. They are designed to push you out of normalcy and out of your comfort zone. You might have to fight through a few days. The demands of everyday life may pull on you, drawing you back into self-consumption. But don't allow those demands to cause you to give up and develop the attitude that this is not important enough to continue. Let me assure you with words that Jesus spoke: *"Greater love has no man than this, that a man lay down his life for his friends"* (John 15:13).

Here Is Your Challenge:

1. For the next 31 days: pray, post, tweet, text, email or phone-in a prayer for another sister. The choice is yours. Each day begins with a scripture reference, summary, and ends with a prayer for you to pray. You can participate in the challenge by yourself or with a group. You can even join the PrayHers 31-Day Challenge on Facebook and enjoy the challenge with friends and family around the world. The power of prayer has no boundaries.

Ideally, you should participate for 31 consecutive days, but if you miss a day for some reason, don't fall out of the race; get back up and keep going. Why 31 days? If you are like me, you have probably spent enough time already being self-consumed, so giving 31 days of your life for the sake of others may be exactly what you need to move your life to the next level. Besides, it takes time to develop a new way of thinking.

2. **Who should I pray for?** Trust me. There is no shortage of people to pray for. Pray for a woman who has the same purpose or calling as you. Instead of treating her like she's competition, treat her like she's an ally. PrayHer success and you will reap your success. You may want to be a fashion designer, so find a designer that you admire and pray for that person. If you want to be a writer, pray for your favorite author. If there is someone you are at odds with, pray for them! The Bible admonishes us to love our enemies and pray for those who despitefully use us (Matthew 5:44, paraphrased).

   You can pray for the same person daily or a different person each day. You can also pray for a celebrity who may be struggling with an addiction or troubled relationship. Instead of sitting back while the media makes a spectacle of her, pray as if she were your friend or family member, because she hurts no differently than the rest of us.

3. **What should I pray?** Oftentimes, people don't pray because they believe they don't know how or what to pray. Prayer is simply a conversation with God. What makes prayer powerful and effective is when you pray according to what God has promised us in the Bible. The prayers that are written at the end of each day are all Bible-based prayers. Read each of them as though it came from your own heart. You can also add in your own words, in addition to what is written. Pray for her peace, direction,

and for her business and relationships. Pray that God watches over her and keeps her in good health.

Some days have an "Extra Step." The extra step may require you to do something for another person or may challenge you to think and examine your heart. The purpose for that is to challenge you further.

Are you ready to make the commitment to give unselfishly of your time and attention for the next 31 days? I think I heard you loudly say, "Yes!" As you journey through this challenge, expect to grow more compassionate and sensitive to the needs of others.

My dear sister, I want to say thank you in advance for your commitment to *PrayHers*. God Bless You!

PRAY HERS

*"And the Lord said, Simon, Simon, behold, Satan hath
desired to have you, that he may sift you as wheat:
But I have prayed for thee, that thy faith fail not: and
when thou are converted, strengthen thy brethren"*
(**Luke 22:31-32**).

If satan could have and destroy us all, he would. But that's
not going to happen, because we are praying women. Jesus
was not ignorant of satan's devices and neither are we (see
2 Corinthians 2:11). Whether we realize it or not, God will
always try to prepare us for what is to come. That's what
Jesus was trying to do for Simon Peter, He was cautioning
him of the test ahead. But Simon responded like most of
us. He ignored the warning. Jesus tried to tell him, *"Before
the cock crows you will deny me three times"* (Luke 22:34). But
Simon Peter, not aware of his own weakness, had a ride or
die attitude (Luke 22:33). In other words, he was adamant
that he would stick with Jesus through thick and thin.

Simon Peter learned a very valuable lesson that day—you
don't always know how you are going to respond in the face
of test and trial until it comes your way. Simon folded during
the sifting process and denied Jesus three times. When the
cock crowed, it sounded an alarm that woke Simon Peter

up to the error of his ways. Scripture tells us that Peter wept bitterly. He was grief-stricken, disgusted, and discouraged because he defaulted on the promise he had made to Jesus. But all hope was not lost, because if you'll recall, Jesus said to him, *I prayed for you.* The way out of Simon's pit of disappointment and failure was already paved through the prayers of Jesus. He prayed that Simon would maintain his faith. Why? Because faith gives us strength to fight our way out of any battle or setback, so that we can reach our destiny.

In the latter part of verse 32, Jesus issued Simon Peter a challenge—similar to the one you are embarking on. He said, *when thou are converted, strengthen thy brethren.* My interpretation goes like this: once you get your life back on track and in the direction God intended, reach back and grab the hand of your sister, don't leave her behind. PrayHers.

Prayer:

Father, I pray that I will always be available to answer the call to pray. Help me to not take the power that I bring into the lives of others lightly and the ramifications that may occur as a result of me ignoring prayer opportunities. If I am falling short, let the cock crow as a reminder to obey You. Help me to continue believing in Your power to deliver me and other women out of difficult situations. Help me to be confident in approaching You on behalf of others, not being intimidated by not knowing what to pray. I trust that You will put the words in my mouth and provide me with the strength to pull my sister out of the pit. In Jesus' name I pray, AMEN!

The Extra Step: Call a friend and ask if she has a prayer request and then take the time to pray immediately for her prayer need. Don't delay!

How Can I Help?

"Those of us who are strong and able in the faith need to step up and lend a hand to those who falter, and not just do what is most convenient for us. Strength is for service, not status. Each one of us needs to look after the good of the people around us, asking ourselves, 'How can I help?' That's exactly what Jesus did. He didn't make it easy for Himself by avoiding people's troubles, but waded right in and helped them out. 'I took on the troubles of the troubled,' is the way Scripture puts it" (**Romans 15:1-3** *MSG*).

I f you happen to be a woman who's ever served in the military then perhaps the Soldier's Creed, "I Will Never Leave a Fallen Comrade," resonates with you. The oath, to never leave a comrade, is a military pledge among soldiers. They view themselves as ONE unit. If one of their own gets hurt in battle, they are not left behind. No! They are picked up and carried to safety by the team.

PrayHers tagline is, *Never Leave a Sister Behind.* When

a sister is going through a battle or struggle in her life, pledge to never leave her side. Pray her through, because there may come a time when you'll find yourself on the battlefield in need of HER help. When you are weak she can be strong for you. It's called working together. So be mindful of the women that you come in contact with today. Take a moment and ask at least one of them, "How can I help you?"

Prayer:

Father God, I pray for_____. I ask that You surround her with women who will speak positive words of encouragement into her life and who will encourage her to achieve the dreams that You have placed on the inside of her. Let her never feel alone in the battles that she faces. Instead, assure her that You have equipped an army of women to come alongside her to hold her up in her times of weakness. Invigorate her mind, body, and soul so that she can be strong enough to help another sister who is weak. In Jesus' name I pray, Amen!

The Extra Step: Today, call a sister and ask her, "How can I help you?" Ask about her well-being. Find out if there is something you can do to lighten her load. Then do it!

Don't Be Ashamed.
Be Healed!

"Confess your faults one to another, and pray one for another, that ye may be healed. The effectual fervent prayer of a righteous [wo]man availeth much" **(James 5:16,** *emphasis added).*

D
on't worry, it's not required that you call up the girls and confess every sin. I believe the writer was referring to the need to be transparent. One of the reasons I believe Joyce Meyer is so effective in her ministry is because she *is* transparent. She is not ashamed of her imperfections, her previous smoking addiction, her previous divorce, or the sexual abuse she encountered as a child. Her transparency and prayer for others has opened the door, not just to her deliverance, but for others as well.

Confessing your faults can be likened to a simple prayer request. What are you in need of? What do you want your sister to petition God about on your behalf? Are you struggling with an addiction? A relationship? A health issue? What are you willing to confess that she may pray?

Also, ask your sister what are *her* specific prayer needs. Although, we can pray general prayers for each other, our prayers are much more targeted and heartfelt when we can pray with specifics. The power that is made available when we pray for each other brings about individual healing. Therefore, don't be ashamed to ask for prayer and don't hesitate to pray for others because that is where healing, deliverance, and freedom lie.

Prayer:

Father God, today I pray for_____. Whatever her struggle is, I ask that You will deliver her from it. I pray that her mind is sound and her soul is at peace. I pray that she will not worry about her life, finances, family, career, or any past sin she has committed. Let her heart be fixed upon trusting in You. Free her from the clutches of public opinion. Help her to reach out for help without concern of embarrassment or ridicule. Remind her that she is forgiven and will always be loved by You. In Jesus' name I pray, Amen!

The Extra Step: Today, if you are struggling with any hurts in your life, albeit physical or emotional, pray for a sister who you know is currently in or has gone through a similar trial. Take your mind off of your situation and allow hers to take first place. Or, call-up a sister, different from the one in Day 2, and ask if she has any specific prayer needs, share with her your own prayer need, and then pray one for another.

DAY
4

BETTER THAN YOUR BARRENNESS

*"There was a man from Ramathaim Zophim, from
the hill country of Ephraim, whose name was Elkanah…He had two wives; the name of the first was
Hannah and the name of the second was Peninnah.
Now Peninnah had children, but Hannah was childless…Her rival wife used to upset her and make her
worry, for the LORD had not enabled her to have
children…Finally her husband Elkanah said to her,
'Hannah, why do you weep and not eat? Why are you
so sad? Am I not better to you than ten sons?'"*
(1 Samuel 1:1a, 2, 6, 8 NET).

annah was a woman who felt a tremendous amount of
sadness over her inability to conceive children. As the
years passed by, Hannah watched in disappointment
as Peninnah paraded along with her children in tow. Every child born to Peninnah was a stake through Hannah's
heart and a reminder of her barrenness. She felt incom-
plete, empty, and embarrassed because she was childless.
And to add insult to injury, Peninnah constantly rubbed

7

it in her face, making her feel less of a woman. But notice what Hannah's husband asked her in a last-ditch effort to comfort her, "Am I not better to you than ten sons?" In other words, he was saying, "Hannah, I'm so good to you. I alone should be enough for you!"

What if God asked you a similar question: "Am I not better to you than anything else you desire?" How would you respond?

Is there anything in your life that you have made greater than God? Sure, your situation may be different from Hannah's and you may already have children, but perhaps you don't have a job right now. Your barrenness may be that you currently don't have a husband, a car, a home, or enough money in the bank. Whatever it is, do not allow it to consume you more than the love of your heavenly Father.

Did Hannah have a baby? Yes, but that didn't happen until she was no longer consumed by her desire. God became first place in her life. As a result of her time in prayer, she made a promise to God that if He granted her a son, she would give him back to Him as a servant (1 Samuel 1:11, 22). Hannah reached a point in her life where God was enough, and whatever she had He could have, even if it meant giving up her greatest treasure.

Like Hannah, you have to come to a place where God is good enough for you, where He means more to you than 10 sons, 10 cars, 10 homes, or even ONE husband. Exodus 20:3 says, "*Thou shalt have no other gods before me.*" So allow God to be better than your barrenness. Give your desires over to Him and watch Him birth the desires of your heart into your life.

Prayer:

Who do you know with a desire so strong that it's consuming them to the point of unhappiness?

Pray these words:

Father God, help _____ to cast the whole of her care upon You, knowing that You care for her. Assure her that no weapon formed against her shall prosper and every tongue rising against her will be silenced. Grant her patience to wait on Your timing. *Let patience have her perfect work, that she may be perfect and entire, wanting nothing* (James 1:4). Let her find joy in serving You and being a daughter of the Most High. Let her not grow weary, lose hope, or give up on what You have promised her. Teach her not to get caught up with time, but with the Father of time who knows how to deliver in due season. Show her how to allow Your grace to be sufficient for her as she learns how to wait. In Jesus' name I pray, Amen!

No Extra Step Today!

LOVE HER ANYWAY

*"But I say unto you, Love your enemies, bless them
[her] that curse you, do good to them [her] that hate
you, and pray for them [her] which despitefully use
you, and persecute you; That ye may be the children of
your Father which is in heaven: for he maketh his sun
to rise on the evil and on the good, and sendeth rain
on the just and on the unjust"* (**Matthew 5:44-45**).

There is nothing more difficult than to speak a kind
word or do a nice deed for a sister who has lied on you,
stolen from you, betrayed you, or used and abused you.
She is someone that you don't want to have anything to
do with, and as far as you're concerned, you don't ever have
to speak her name again. But wait! After all she's done to
hurt you, Jesus has the audacity to issue a command that
you are to *love her anyway*! And in the same breath, ask
you to...What! Pray for her?

To the natural mind, this seems backwards and crazy.
You almost want to say, "Jesus, don't you mean slap her

across the face and then pray she doesn't press charges?" Not quite! Another person's behavior will never alter God's position on walking in love. When you can "Love her anyway," despite all the pain she's caused, you are proving that you are God's daughter and that you are able to shine His love on the good and the bad.

Prayer:

Think of a woman who has betrayed you and right now, pray for her.

Father God, I thank You for_____ I ask that You provide every need in her life today. I ask You to excuse anything or anyone in her life that is preventing her from drawing closer to You. If there is any hurt in her heart that may have provoked her betrayal, please mend it with Your love. Help her to treat even **her** enemies with kindness and respect, not repaying evil for evil. Let Your love rule in her heart so that her enemies can see Your good work in her and glorify Your name. In Jesus' name I pray, Amen!

The Extra Step: Do a kind deed for a person who has angered you in anyway (Ouch!). You might call that taking a double step!

DAY
6

GET RID OF THE UNFORGIVE-MESS

"Therefore I say unto you, what things soever ye desire, when ye pray, believe that ye receive [them] and ye shall have [them]. And when ye stand praying, forgive, if ye have ought against any: that your Father also which is in heaven may forgive you your trespasses" (**Mark 11:24-25**).

*B*asketball Wives...*Real Housewives of Atlanta*...*Real Housewives of Miami*...What words come to your mind as you read off the names of those reality television shows? How about drama? catfight? jealousy? scandal? Sum it all up and you have... a big MESS! Doesn't it seem like mess gravitates towards women, forcing us into being at odds and in unforgiveness with one another? The reality of it is this: we tend to hold the hurts in our heart until they manifest into anger, envy, hatred, bitterness, or insecurity; all of these feelings are blockades to healing and answered prayer. With that being the case, you have to ask yourself, "Is whatever she did or said worth my peace of mind?" Is it worth coming between you and God...

because that's what happens when you stand in a pile of *unforgive-mess.*

Keep the passageway to your heart clear. Your heart affects how you believe and receive from God. He has so much He wants to get to you, but it is required that you have a forgiving heart. If you will forgive her faults, God will forgive yours. Don't allow the accuser, satan, to accuse your sister before you. Forgive! Trust me. It's the best thing for you, because before you know it, you are going to be in the need of forgiveness yourself. Right now, search your heart for ought against any sister and release it.

Prayer:

God, I love You and I enjoy the fellowship that I have with You. I don't want anything to interfere with that. I ask that You help me to search my heart for any unforgiveness that may reside. I pray that my heart has a direct link to the desires You have for my life. I make a decision today to pray for_____ I pray that her heart is clear of any unforgiveness toward me or any other person, so that she can receive the many blessings that You have for her. Grant her peace, love, and tranquility all the days of her life and fill her soul with joy. In Jesus' name I pray, Amen!

The Extra Step: If while searching your heart you discovered that you have unforgiveness toward someone, call them and apologize. Don't concern yourself with their response, because the response you desire is not guaranteed. Remember, this is a decision of the heart and a blazoned step toward expressing your love for God. All you have to do is make known your willingness to forgive them, and then sit back and watch peace flood your life.

In Hers Is Yours

"And it came to pass, that, when Elisabeth heard the salutation of Mary, the babe leaped in her womb; and Elisabeth was filled with the Holy Ghost: And she spake out with a loud voice, and said, Blessed art thou among women, and blessed is the fruit of thy womb"
(Luke 1:41-42).

I have in my mind a picture of two high-spirited women, both thrilled to be pregnant, who when they saw each other their faces lit up with excitement, smiles, and genuine love for each other. All Mary did was greet Elisabeth, possibly a simple *hello*, but that alone was enough to impart great joy into Elisabeth's life. In return, Elisabeth then declared a blessing over Mary's life by saying, *"Blessed art thou among women, and blessed is the fruit of thy womb."*

The love inside of Mary brought joy inside of Elisabeth. Likewise, the gift on the inside of you can stir something on the inside of *HER*. Never underestimate the power you bring into another woman's life. That's why it's important to live in forgiveness and not in strife. Great power is made available when women come together in unity and love, and celebrate the dreams and visions other women carry inside their wombs.

Don't undervalue what you bring to the table and what you're able to help birth out of your sister. God has called us to *PrayHers* in order to get ours. I declare, like Elisabeth, with a loud shout, "WOMAN THOU ARE BLESSED!!!" You are blessed to be a blessing. Everything you set your hands to will bring forth good fruit.

Prayer:

Father, I pray for every woman I come in contact with today. I ask that You would allow me to impart something into them that will brighten their day or change their lives for the better, whether it's a smile, a word of encouragement, a prayer, or a simple hello. Let me be the one to help birth out their dreams. Whatever You have given me, I ask that You use it to help my sisters get theirs. In Jesus' name I pray, Amen!

The Extra Step: Purpose today to bring a smile to a sister's face. Compliment a clerk while you are out at the store shopping.

GREAT vs. GREAT

*"But the angel said unto him, Fear not, Zacharias:
for thy prayer is heard; and thy wife Elisabeth shall
bear thee **a son**, and thou shalt call his name JOHN.
For he shall be GREAT in the sight of the Lord...
And he shall go before him [the Lord] in the spirit and
power of Elias, to turn the hearts of the fathers to the
children, and the disobedient to the wisdom of the just;
to make ready a people prepared for the Lord"*
(Luke 1:13, 15, 17, *emphasis added).*

*The angel talking to Mary said, "And, behold, thou
shalt conceive in thy womb, and bring forth **a son**,
and shalt call his name JESUS. He shall be GREAT,
and shall be called the Son of the Highest: and the
Lord God shall give unto him the throne of his father
David."* **(Luke 1:31-32**, *emphasis added).*

Mary and Elisabeth BOTH received a word from the angel that their sons would be GREAT! Did they go into competition mode and begin to compare their sons to one another? No. Did it matter to them whose son would be greater? No. Should it matter to us who will be greater amongst women? No! John the Baptist embraced his role as the one who was to announce the coming of Jesus Christ. He even referred to Jesus as being mightier than him. John did not feel threatened, insecure, or less important just because he was not the Savior of the world. He was still a great man, respected by many.

Sometimes our role is simply to make room for other people and to help them walk in their gifts. Oftentimes, God will have us do things in order to help prepare the way for our sister. John did it for Jesus and we must not be too prideful, selfish, or fearful that our own dreams won't come to pass that we fail to follow the example given to us by God.

God has called us ALL to be GREAT! The Greek word for GREAT is MEGAS, which means that we're all MEGA-Women. That's why we don't need to envy or compare ourselves to each other. Great is Great. If I'm called to sweep floors and you're called to own and operate a million dollar company, so be it. I should strive to be the best floor sweeper the world has ever seen and you should strive to be the best business owner alive! We both experience the same level of GREATNESS, because we're both operating in our roles and God can't do anything less than great. Whatever God has ordained for you, it is for you and it is great. Celebrate what God has called you and the women in your life to do. Don't ever think or be afraid that God has made you insignificant. There is enough greatness in God to fill ALL of us.

Prayer:

Father, today I pray for_____. Help her to see that she is indeed already great. Help her to learn her purpose in life so that there's no confusion or doubt about why she is here. Help her to be confident in her own abilities so that there is no need for comparison. Help her to be comfortable around other great women without feeling envious, jealous, or insecure. Lord, I pray that all women would recognize and appreciate our uniqueness and realize that in You we can be nothing less than GREAT! In Jesus' name, I submit this prayer, AMEN!

The Extra Step: Sow a seed of time or finances into the dream of another sister. It doesn't matter how big or small as long as it's from the heart. Help her, in whatever way you can, to grow her vision, because ultimately it affects you.

EACH ONE REACH ONE

"All praise to the God and Father of our Master, Jesus the Messiah! Father of all mercy! God of all healing counsel! He comes alongside us when we go through hard times, and before you know it, he brings us alongside someone else who is going through hard times so that we can be there for that person just as God was there for us" (**2 Corinthians 1:3-4** *MSG)*.

How many times have you looked at another sister and thought to yourself: "Her life seems so perfect. She's polished, successful, confident, and in control. She doesn't have a care in the world. I wish that were me"? If we are honest with ourselves, most of us would admit to those thoughts. However, what we don't realize is that what we're doing is seeking her glory without knowing her story.

Rewind back the time and you will see that she was once in a very abusive relationship that robbed her of the attributes you now admire. For years she struggled through insecurity, lowliness, and self-hatred. And if she were to allow you a sneak peek into her heart, you may be surprised to find that at times…she still has to fight off the demons of her past.

So often we look at the outer things of women—their cars, perfectly manicured nails, neat hair, designer clothes, and outward beauty—without looking at what's on the inside of them and what they've had to overcome. We are unaware of their true stories, the stories that helped form who they are today.

Everyone goes through trials and challenging times, just like the Bible says, *"There's nothing new under the sun" (Ecclesiastes 1:9)*. Think about the most difficult and trying time you have faced in your life, but overcame it. Think about the hurt and pain you felt during that time. Chances are there is a sister going through the exact same or similar situation today, experiencing the same hurt and pain you did. What better person to help her through than you? Someone out there is looking at your glory, but they don't know your story. You can help someone else overcome!

Something you may face tomorrow is being conquered by a sister today. Hopefully, she will be there for you like you have the chance to be there for someone right now. If each one reaches one, no one will be left behind.

Prayer:

God of comfort, today I pray for_____. You know the secret compartments of her heart. You know her weaknesses and her fears. Today, I ask that You strengthen her where she is weak. Let her not lose heart or give up on herself or You. I pray that she has a righteous boldness to stand against doubt and unbelief. Give her victory over all her test and trials, enemies, and naysayers. In Jesus' name I pray, Amen!

No Extra Step Today!

DON'T BE A DISCOURAGEHER

*"Whither shall we go up? our brethren have dis-
couraged our heart, saying, The people is greatH-
ER and tallHER than we; the cities are great
and walled up to heaven; and moreover we have
seen the sons [daughters] of the Anakims there"*
(**Deuteronomy 1:28**, *emphasis added*).

At times the biggest and most difficult mountain to overcome is discouragement. Why? Because often-times discouragement comes by way of those we love and admire, those whose opinion we esteem highly. We turn their fears, insecurities, and doubts into our own—robbing ourselves of future dreams. We compare ourselves to the greatness of others and assume we can't measure up. Or, we will discontinue our dream simply because we see another person already doing the same thing. I encourage you not to look at another person's qualifications, resources, abilities, or achievements to determine whether or not you qualify to have your own. No matter how insurmountable your goals may appear—they are reachable.

Don't be discouraged by naysayers, and for goodness sake, *don't be the naysayer!* Choose your words wisely when giving sisterly advice. If you don't agree with HER, then take it to God in prayer and allow Him to deal with her concerning her dreams and desires. After all, who's to say that you're right? She may very well be on the path that God has chosen for her. Don't stop her from her next-level opportunity just because her dream seems impossible or out-of-the-way in your eyes. Remember that with God, ALL things are possible for you...and her!

Prayer:

Father, I pray that my words are always seasoned with love and compassion toward my sisters. Let not my lips be the cause of her abandoning her dreams. Give me the words to say that will encourage her without my opinion or thoughts getting in the way. Help me to know when to listen and when to speak and when to listen and keep my mouth closed. I pray that my sister will not be discouraged by the successes or failures of others. I pray that she doesn't feel the need to compete against anyone. Help her to see that through You she can, indeed, do ALL things—no matter how big or small they may be. In Jesus' name I pray, Amen!

The Extra Step: Today, send a word of encouragement to another sister: perhaps a famous quote, your own words, or favorite scripture. Go ahead! Be an encourageHER.

WONDERFULLY MADE

"I will praise thee; for I am fearfully and wonderfully made: marvellous are thy works; and that my soul knoweth right well" (**Psalm 139:14**).

When India.Arie appeared on the music scene with her song, "Video," she arrived with a strong message for young girls and women with insecurities such as: low self-esteem and a less than perfect body image. Her message helped us to be able to look in the mirror and say, *"What God gave me is just fine."*

"Video" Lyrics excerpt:
*I'm not the average girl from your video
And I ain't built like a supermodel.
But, I learned to love myself unconditionally,
Because I am a queen
I'm not the average girl from your video
My worth is not determined by the price of my clothes.
No matter what I'm wearing I will always be
India.Arie*

*[Verse 2]
When I look in the mirror and the only one there is me
Every freckle on my face is where it's supposed to be*

And I know my creator didn't make no mistakes on me
My feet, my thighs, my Lips, my eyes, I'm loving what I see

How many of us can say that we love ourselves unconditionally? Unfortunately, not very many; we are constantly picking ourselves apart, always finding something dissatisfying. We tell ourselves that we are not pretty enough, we have the wrong body shape, or we're too short or too tall. But these things are not true! We were made beautiful and it's time to own it! So let the words of India.Arie's song become your anthem. When you look in the mirror, LOVE what you see. Learn to love yourself unconditionally. After all, we are ALL queens and we are all valuable.

Challenge yourself to not compare yourself to other women, instead celebrate your uniqueness and love the fact you were FEARFULLY and WONDERFULLY MADE BY GOD.

Prayer:

Father God, Creator of woman, I pray for_____.
Teach my sister to love herself like You love her. Remind her daily that she was made to be different. You meant for her to stand out. When she looks in the mirror help her to say, "I am beautiful and brilliant, and I love what I see."

Father God, show Your queen that the price of her clothes, the car that she drives, the house that she lives in, or all the money in the world will NEVER be more valuable than her, because she is fearfully and wonderfully made. In Your son Jesus' name I pray, Amen!

The Extra Step: Today share with another sister what you most admire about her. What makes her unique? Celebrate the qualities that make her who she is. The challenge is on.

DO IT AS UNTO THE LORD!

*"And whatsoever ye do, do it heartily, as to the Lord,
and not unto [wo]men;"* (**Colossians 3:23**).

Years ago I attended a conference where a speaker, by the name of Bunny Wilson, spoke. She said something that I will never forgot—"If you love without expectation, you break the power over individuals to hurt you." How many times have you shown kindness to someone only to get a response different from what you expected? Not a thank you, great job, or I appreciate you.

Anyone who has poured blood, sweat, and tears into anything will understand that feeling of disappointment and frustration, when you don't get the response or results that you anticipated. Or, all of your effort seems to go unnoticed and unappreciated.

NEWS ALERT: Everyone won't think what you are doing is wonderful or that you are wonderful. People will dislike you for no reason other than they just don't like you and you have to be willing to accept it and move on. But that's when you must take a moment to examine your motives. You ask yourself the question. Am I doing this for man's approval or God's? Am I trying to be seen of men, or be seen of God?

Oftentimes, we do things to gain attention and approval of man. We measure our success by numbers, approval ratings, opinions, and "likes." I am not saying that indicators are not important. They definitely help gauge a response to your efforts, but what if the indicators don't meet your expectation? Does that mean you are a failure? Does it mean it's time to throw in the towel and give up? Not when you do it for God! Not when your heart and motive is to serve Him. *And whatsoever ye do, do [it] heartily, as to the Lord, and not unto men; Knowing that of the Lord ye shall receive the reward of the inheritance: for ye serve the Lord Christ. (Colossians 3:23-24).*

Prayer:

Father God, I pray for _____. Reveal to her the motives of her heart, so that whatever she does, it's for the sole purpose of honoring You. Teach her to love, forgive, and pray for those she deems ungrateful. Help her to look to You instead of those around her for the accolades she desires. I declare that my sister will forsake the opinions of others in exchange to be a God-pleaser. In Jesus' name I pray, Amen!

The Extra Step: From this day forward, whatever you do, purpose to do it from your heart, not so that you can be seen or appreciated. Expect your thank you(s), appreciation, and rewards to come from God and God alone.

U-N-I-T-Y

"The way God designed our bodies is a model for
understanding our lives together as a church: every
part dependent on every other part, the parts we men-
tion and the parts we don't, the parts we see and the
parts we don't. If one part hurts, every other part is
involved in the hurt, and in the healing. If one part
flourishes, every other part enters into the exuberance"
(1 Corinthians 12:25-26 *MSG).*

All the different parts that make up your body—your eyes, legs, arms …—belong to your *one* body. Wouldn't it be foolish to be jealous because your ears don't see? I am quite certain you don't feel slighted because your ears don't think. Aren't you more effective as a whole when ALL of your parts are functioning the way they were created? That is the same attitude we must learn to develop amongst each other. Those of us who believe that Jesus Christ is the Savior of the world become part of ONE body of believers. Therefore, it is foolish for us to look at each other sideways with envy, jealousy, or opposition simply because we have different callings or assignments.

When we function together, the way we were created and not covet other positions, we are more effective, more powerful, and more beautiful.

We are divinely connected. God has equipped us ALL to play a special part in each other's lives. So let's not fail each other, but let's pray for one another in unity.

Prayer:

Father God, help me to do my part in creating a united front with the women around me. May I value her worth and uplift her in her gifts and calling. Help me to see her as an ally and not as my enemy. Help us join forces for Your glory. I pray a hedge of protection over everything that concerns her knowing that it affects me as well. In Jesus' name, I declare unity with my sisters, Amen!

No Extra Step Today!

RESTORE HER

B ishop George Davis, Pastor of Faith Christian Center in Jacksonville, FL wrote an article in an on-line magazine that I thought was perfect for this challenge. It reads:

It is our job to bring others back to a position of peace—the place of total wholeness or completeness—where nothing is broken, spirit, soul or body. There are so many people in this world that are hurting. Some are discouraged, disgusted and walking around with feelings of condemnation because they have gotten off track and feel like they cannot come back home to Christ. It is the believer's job to share with them that it is never too late to return. There is never a time where they have gotten so far away from God that He won't welcome them back. Be the one that has a heart to run after those who are out of fellowship with God. Endeavor to speak a word of compassionate encouragement that will restore them to a position of oneness again.[1]

---

1 Davis, G. L.(April, 24, 2012). Leave No Man Behind. *Faith Leaders*. Retrieved March 6, 2014, from http://faithleaders.com/articles/2012/04/leave-no-man-behind.

Indeed, many women are hurting right now for various reasons. Some are hurt due to a failed relationship, the death of a loved one, not being able to conceive a child, or because they lack purpose in life. And because of pride, a woman might be too ashamed to let others in on how she is feeling, which is why we must be sensitive and aware of the clues that she could be giving off. Perhaps she doesn't smile as much or she beats herself up with regret. Ask God to give you the right words to bring this sister out of the clutches of despair.

God says that He will never leave nor forsake us. Jesus illustrates this principle through the parables of the shepherd leaving the 99 sheep to find the one sheep that had gone astray. A hurting sister needs to know that she is cared about and that God has not forgotten her. Remind her what God says, *"But even if mothers forget, I'd never forget you—never.* (Isaiah 49:15b-16 MSG). She may be reluctant to believe you at first, so you may even have to state the obvious: "God had you on His mind, when He placed you on my heart today."

Don't ignore the signs of a sister in distress and leave her to fend for herself. She needs you. God has given you boldness and courage to help restore her joy.

Prayer:

Father God, I pray for every woman that I know who may be hurting right now. I realize that at times we may be too prideful and ashamed of the storms that we are facing in our own lives, and because of this, we don't reach out for help. If my sister is too embarrassed to open up and reach out for help, I pray that You free her from any shame she may be experiencing. Help her to clearly understand that true freedom is in her transparency and that it is okay to ask for help. Some of us spend a great deal of time, resources, and energy being there for others that we have become weak in our own fight. I ask You to restore her and gird her up with Your full armor. I pray that her mind is clear to think positively and receive all that You have destined for her life. In Jesus' name I pray, Amen!

The Extra Step: Call a sister and assure her of God's love for her. Let her know that God is thinking about her and that He has a plan for her future. No matter who we are and what we have accomplished, it's always a welcoming pleasure to know that we are loved.

The Halfway Mark!

Don't Get Weary

"Anyone who meets a testing challenge head-on and manages to stick it out is mighty fortunate. For such persons loyally in love with God, the reward is life and more life" (**James 1:12** *MSG).*

Challenges are not made to be easy or convenient; they demand our time and effort. But guess what! You are halfway through the challenge, the point where most people get weary and want to give up, thinking, "What's the point of this anyway?" But I say to you: Don't you dare give up! Your sister needs you; her life may just depend on you sticking this challenge out for just two more weeks.

You have the power to impact lives. Keep in mind, we are all in this together and by doing our individual parts, we collectively keep the body in tip-top shape. Giving up on her now is the same as giving up on you. Don't underestimate your worth and what you have to offer. No matter how big or small your assignment, it's needed! So don't get weary... continue on.

Prayer:

Father, I pray for every sister right now who has made a decision to partake in the PrayHers 31-Day Challenge. Give her the willingness to continue through to the end, despite the temptation to be drawn away by other things that are demanding her time and attention. I know that You are faithful not to forget her labor of love that she has shown and sown towards other women (Hebrews 6:10). What she is doing is pleasing to You, which positions her to receive from You her own desires. Thank You for the opportunity to take selfishness head-on, as she continues to serve the needs of others in prayer. In Jesus' name, we honor and thank You, Amen!

The Extra Step: If you are sharing this challenge with another sister, encourage each other to continue on. Share with each other how the challenge has helped you.

The Reward of a Heart that Esteems Others

God: *"What can I give you?*

Solomon: *"Wisdom and knowledge to judge YOUR people.*

God: *"...Because this was in thine heart, and thou hast not asked riches, wealth, or honour, nor the life of thine enemies, neither yet hast asked long life; but hast asked wisdom and knowledge for thyself, that thou mayest judge my people, over whom I have made thee king: Wisdom and knowledge is granted unto thee; and I will give thee riches, and wealth, and honour, such as none of the kings have had that have been before thee, neither shall there any after thee have the like"* (**2 Chronicles 1:11-12**).

I f God asked you, "What can I give you?" what would your response be? a new car? a house? a husband? money? Many of us would probably have our personal agendas on our minds first, but not Solomon. He was more concerned about being a blessing to others than he was with getting his needs and desires met. He asked God for wisdom to lead *His* people. Because of this, Solomon got exceeding, abundantly, above, and beyond what he could ask or think (Ephesians 3:20), including money and things. Solomon's *heart* was in the right place.

Pure hearts ask with the right motives and right motives receive pure blessings. When you pray for others, ask God to give you a pure heart to pray. Ask Him to reveal areas of impurity so that when you go before God on HER behalf, not only will God oblige you, but He will in turn grant you exceedingly, abundantly, above, and beyond what you can ask or think. God's way of getting is to FIRST give. You have to give away what you desire to have. Praying for others IS giving. Be more concerned about others and less concerned about status and things.

Prayer:

Lord, I pray against selfish thinking. Help my mind and my heart to be more concerned with the needs of my sister instead of being consumed with my own desires. Give me the words to pray as I petition You on her behalf. I give You permission to access my soul and touch my heart to give of my time and resources in order to be a blessing to my sister. I ask for an understanding heart that I may value my sisters who are all important to You. In Jesus' name I pray, Amen!

The Extra Step: Ask God to help you examine your heart for wrong motives that may be lurking. Take a look at your involvements and ask yourself, "Why I am doing this?"

DAY
17

WHOSE ESTHER ARE YOU?

Esther was a Jewish woman who lost both of her parents. She was then taken in by her uncle, Mordecai. When Mordecai heard that King Ahasuerus was looking for a new queen, he presented Esther as a prospect. She was amongst a large pool of women who all had hopes of being the next queen. After a lengthy selection process, the king chose Esther as his new queen.

After Esther was named queen, the king okayed a decree to kill all Jews, not knowing Queen Esther was a Jew. Mordecai was terrified and wanted Esther to ask her husband to put a stop to it. Mordecai says in the Scripture, *"Don't imagine that because you are part of the king's household you will be the one Jew who will escape. If you keep quiet at this time, liberation and protection for the Jews will appear from another source, while you and your father's household perish. It may very well be that you have achieved royal status for such a time as this!"* (**Esther 4:13-14** NET).

EstHER's promotion to royalty wasn't just so that she can wear fine clothes and dine in fine places or enjoy the privilege of not lifting a finger to do work. Esther's promotion to queen had a much greater purpose that benefited more than just her; it was for the benefit of protecting an entire nation. Once Esther realized this, she was willing to lay down her life for her Jewish nation (see Esther 4:16). And because she was willing, not only did she spare her own life and save the Jews from extinction, but her favor with the King positioned her uncle Mordecai to be promoted from gate keeper to a royal ruler.

Whose EstHER are you? Who are you here for? Who is God using you to promote? You are here for the Master's use. If you make yourself available to God, He will put you in places you never dreamed of. He doesn't place you there so that you can become prideful and conceited, but so that you can be available to open doors for others. Don't take it lightly that you have committed 31 days of your life to pray for other women. God is protecting your future too, just like He did for the Jews. The women you are praying for may very well be the ones God will promote for the purpose of promoting you. The woman you have found yourself envious of may be the one woman chosen to set you up for your time in the spotlight. So the next time you are tempted to envy, backbite, or belittle another sister, you may want to ask yourself this question, "Is that my EstHER?"

Prayer:

Father God, today I make myself available to You. I humbly accept whatever status or position You choose to place me in. Help me to recognize my purpose in the lives of the women around me and help them to recognize their purpose in mine. Lord, help us to realize that we are not here to compete, but to complement each other as You see fit. In Jesus' name I pray, Amen!

The Extra Step: Are you mentoring someone? Is anyone mentoring you? Today, ask God what is the purpose of the women in your life, and more importantly, what your purpose in their lives is.

FAITHFULNESS MATTERS

"[S]he that is faithful in that which is least is faithful also in much…And if ye have not been faithful in that which is another [wo]man's, who shall give you that which is your own?" (**Luke 16:10a, 12**).

What words come to mind when you think of someone who is faithful? How about consistent, dedicated, true-blue, selfless, reliable, humble, and loyal? Wow! Who wouldn't want a person with these characteristics on their team and in their corner? A woman who is faithful is just that—faithful. It doesn't matter to her if she will benefit a little, a lot, or not at all. Her job title and position doesn't matter to her either; she's faithful in whatever she puts her hands to. Whether she's a corporate executive or waits tables at a restaurant, she is faithful in everything she does.

How committed are you to what you do, especially what you do for others? Are you able to show the same love and compassion for *hers* as you would your own? Your faithfulness and attitude towards others is what qualifies you to walk in your own blessings. Why…because a faithful heart is priceless in the sight of God. So please, dear sister, don't underestimate the level of faithfulness that you are demonstrating by making the commitment to stay with *The PrayHers 31-Day Challenge.* You will receive great blessings. Your faithfulness matters!

Prayer:

Lord, I simply ask this of You: teach me faithfulness so that no matter what I am doing, big or small, I will do it with a faithful heart, not giving attention to what's in it for me, but focusing on what's in it for You. In Jesus' name I pray, Amen!

The Extra Step: Faithfulness usually results in a lifestyle change, which happens in the heart. Choose at least one area in your life (health, relationships, career, or any other area) where you know requires an unrelenting decision to remain faithful—then do it!

FEAR NOT!

*"I will not be afraid of ten thousands of people, that
have set themselves against me round about"*
(Psalms 3:6).

Whatever it is, don't be afraid of it. Whoever it is, don't be afraid of them. It doesn't matter how BIG the situation may be or how many people seem to be against you, do not be intimidated. Keep moving! Everyone will not be for you, including those you love and care about. As a matter of fact, your greatest opposition may come from those closest to you. Still, keep moving!

Today, purpose not to worry about how the situation is going to work out, what "they" are thinking about you, or how that bill is going to get paid. Whatever the situation that is coming against you—Fear Not! And if you really want to get away from the problem(s), start focusing your attention on the desires of others. Prayer is a seed you sow and you will receive whatever you need from that seed. So again, fear not and start praying for somebody else.

Prayer:

Father, I pray for_____. I know there is nothing or no one that is bigger than You. It doesn't matter who is against her as long as You are for her. If David can take out a 9-feet giant, named Goliath, then surely_____ can take out the giants in her life with the power that is in Your word. I pray now that You will fill her mouth with words of faith that will slay the giants and knock down the mountains standing in her way. I pray that she'll realize that she is stronger than her adversaries and nothing by any means shall harm her. Strengthen her with Your might and give her victory over her giants. In Jesus' name I pray, Amen!

The Extra Step: What has you the most hesitant or afraid right now? Is it a phone call you need to make or an assignment or person you've avoided? Once you identify what it is, address it. Today! Do not allow fear to stop you.

The Business Woman of the Year

"Who can find a virtuous woman? for her price is far above rubies…She considereth a field, and buyeth it: with the fruit of her hands she planteth a vineyard… She maketh fine linen, and selleth it; and delivereth girdles unto the merchant" (**Proverbs 31:10, 16, 24**)

We hear about her often and many of us aspire to be like her. We read about her and study her. She is well-organized and she can multitask. She is a wife, a mother, and a very successful business woman who specializes in buying real estate. She designs and sells clothing. The Bible says that she plants a vineyard with her own hands, so she isn't afraid of getting her hands dirty. She is up late and out early. She's a woman who demands respect. She manages her success while making sure neither her husband nor her children are neglected in the process. *She looketh well to the ways of her household…Her children arise up, and call her blessed; her husband also, and he praiseth her"* (Proverbs 31: 27a, 28). Who *is* this woman? She *is* the Proverbs 31 woman.

What woman would not love to be this efficient? The problem for many of us is the daunting task of balancing both career and family. We are afraid that in the quest for one, the other will suffer. However, the Proverbs 31 woman clearly proves that women can have it all—great success, a happy family, and be of full joy. If it weren't so, God would not have shown us this woman as a roadmap. So don't be afraid to give it all you've got!

If you are a woman who struggles with the idea of having children because you don't want your career to suffer, then consider the woman you just read about. If you are married or unmarried with children and you are afraid of "dropping the ball" where your family is concerned, you should also consider the Proverbs 31 woman. She proves that it can be done. God is no respecter of persons. If He did it for her, He will do it for you. Just follow the footsteps of the Proverbs 31 woman and you won't miss a beat. Think of a working woman you know and pray for her.

Prayer:

Lord, I pray for_____. Help her to balance her career and her family. I pray that neither she nor her family ever suffers as a result of her pursuing her dreams. Let all things be done decently and in order in her life. Help her not to be anxious or overwhelmed as she attempts to balance all that is before her. I pray that Your great grace rest upon her, giving her the ability to shine while effectively and efficiently running not only her household, but her career. Let all that she sets her hands to—prosper. In Jesus' name I thank You, Amen!

The Extra Step: Bless a sister with the gift of organization today. Buy her a storage bin, a book, or email her a tip you read on how to be better organized. If she's not taking this challenge with you, be sure to let her know that you're blessing her as part of a prayer challenge. Some people take kind gestures the wrong way when they don't know the reason behind them, and we don't want that to happen.

He is No Good...
Without You

"And the LORD God said, It is not good that the man should be alone; I will make him an help meet for him" (**Genesis 2:18**).

ingle ladies, when I was a single woman I would often say, "Lord, You said that it is not good for man to be alone and right now my husband is alone without me and that is not good. We need to meet." And eventually, my knight in shining armor found me.

Married ladies, once you've said, "I do," it's easy to forget about the days of old...being single that is. You forget about those lonely days and how much you desired to spend the holidays with that special someone. You forget about how year after year you showed up to the family reunion just to be bombarded with statements and questions most single people loathe, "When are you going to get married?" or "You're not married yet!" as if something was terribly wrong with you.

For those of us who have already walked down the aisle, let's not forget how difficult some of those single days were. Let's PrayHer strength and patience because it's easy to grow weary and want to jump on the first train that comes by. We don't want her marrying the wrong person or even the right person at the wrong time. Let all the single ladies say, "AMEN."

If you are single with the desire to be married, then I urge you to find yourself married to the Lord first. Be faithful to Him! Be satisfied with His timing, then when you least expect it, your prince will come riding into your life.

Prayer:

Father, I pray for my single friend(s) who desires to be married. Help her not to look at the clock, but exercise patience as she waits on Your timing to be married. Let her be content with being loved by You alone. Give her the willingness and strength to keep herself pure before You. Assure her that there is a man out there looking earnestly for her and that at the right time, You will order his steps in her direction. I pray for her husband-to-be, that he will recognize her as his helpmeet and that he will not be afraid, intimidated, or doubtful of her purpose in his life. In Jesus' name I pray, Amen!

The Extra Step: If there is someone you know who has been waiting eagerly for her husband to come along, reach out to her today and assure her that you are standing in faith with her.

Strong Enough for a Man, but Made a Woman

"For the man is not of the woman: but the woman for the man. Neither was the man created for the woman; but the woman for the man" (**1 Corinthians 11:8-9**).

Yesterday, it was about being single. Today it's about being married. Any married woman will tell you that marriage is a lot of work and that is not a cliché. It is a job that you must become very skilled at or you may find yourself reliving your single days. Oftentimes, strong-willed women or women who have managed to achieve success while single have a harder time adjusting to their positions as wives according to God's definition of a wife. They don't always realize that they were **created** to be suitable and adaptable to their spouses. And as subservient as that may sound, it's true.

A woman who is suitable and adaptable is like a chameleon, she has the ability to be whoever she needs to be for her man. The problem is a lot of women think that adapting robs them of an opinion, independence, and a life. But let's not forget the Proverbs 31 woman (Day 20); she managed to keep her husband happy and herself fulfilled. Women have the awesome power of helping men bring the visions God gave them to past. Women have divine influence. Things happen because a woman is involved.

Prayer:

Father God, I present to You all of my married friends. I pray that all things will be done decently and in order as it pertains to their households. Help my friends to understand and honor the role of wife. I pray that You will help them to understand that they are not inferior, but made to be helpers to the men in their lives. May their marriages flourish and grow to new heights as both of them are fulfilled and satisfied together. In Jesus' name I pray, Amen!

The Extra Step: If you are married, ask your husband if he feels you are a help or motivation to him. Do you know the true desires of his heart? What does he hope to accomplish? Help take something off of his to-do list.

If you are single, pray that your married sisters will have love and joy-filled marriages, just as you desire for yourself one day.

DIVINE CONNECTIONS

"And Elimelech Naomi's husband died; and she was left, and her two sons...And Mahlon and Chilion [her two sons] died also both of them; and the woman was left of her two sons and her husband" (**Ruth 1:3, 5**).

Naomi's husband and her two sons died. Although both sons were married, their wives had not borne any children; therefore, Naomi didn't have any grandchildren. It looked as if this was the end of her husband's lineage. She felt hopeless. The Bible tells us that she told her daughters-in-law that she was too old to marry again and couldn't have sons for them to marry. It would be foolish to even think it would happen, so she admonished both of her daughters to leave her and go on with their lives. They owed her nothing.

One of Naomi's daughters-in-law, Ruth, decided that she was not going to allow her husband's death to disrupt her devotion to her mother-in-law. She chose to stick by Naomi's side. These two together became a Divine Connection.

When Naomi returned to live in her native town, word spread quickly about Ruth's unselfish decision to forsake all and accompany her mother-in-law back home. The news even found its way into the ears of a wealthy single man named Boaz. "[Ruth]… *for all the city of my people doth know that thou art a virtuous woman,*" Boaz said to her (Ruth 3:11). Naomi told Ruth that Boaz was a part of the lineage of their deceased husbands, and if she and Boaz were to marry and have children, their lineage would continue. In other words, death did not have to stop life.

Ruth and Boaz eventually married and had a son named Obed, who became the grandfather of King David. It was from the lineage of King David that Jesus was born. Through Naomi and Ruth's connection, we got Jesus, the Redeemer of our souls. Now that's divine! One could not have done it without the other.

Before you decide to detach yourself from someone, pray and make sure you are not detaching yourself from a divine connection and aborting the future.

Prayer:

Father, I pray for every sister who has dealt with the tragedy of losing a child or husband through death or divorce. I pray that You will give her peace and assurance that her life is not over and that You can turn the situation into a great victory. Remind her that You will never leave her comfortless. Not only will You be there for her, but You will provide a ram in the bush or people who will commit themselves to remaining by her side. I pray that every spiritual, emotional, physical, and financial need in her life is met by Your love and grace. Grant her serenity and joy. In Jesus' name I pray, Amen.

The Extra Step: Do you know anyone who has recently gone through a divorce or death of a loved one? Call them and pray with them today concerning any desire they have.

DON'T BE ASHAMED OF YOUR PRAISE

"And at midnight Paul and Silas prayed, and sang praises unto God: and the prisoners heard them. And suddenly there was a great earthquake, so that the foundations of the prison were shaken: and immediately all the doors were opened, and every one's bands were loosed" (**Acts 16:25-26**).

Do you want to know what excites me the most about Paul and Silas? Well, for the sake of this challenge, let's pretend their names were Paula and Selena. They were not ashamed or concerned about who was around when they got their praise on! They didn't care about what others thought about their crying out to God. They praised Him! It was their prayers and praise that caused the foundation of failure, sickness, insecurity, and fear to be shaken off the lives of the other prisoners. Those prisoners didn't even realize that their own freedom was bound in the praise of someone else.

When Paula and Selena praised, ALL of the prison

doors were opened, not just for them—the two doing all the work—but also for those in the presence of the work. EVERYONE got freed. Are you getting this? Is it starting to sound redundant to you? It's supposed to. I pray that with each new challenge day, the revelation of how interdependent we all are is sinking into the innermost part of your soul. What you do or don't do has an effect on those around you.

What if Paula and Selena had decided to be closet Christians, ashamed and afraid they might offend those in the next cell? They would have remained in bondage. How many people around you are still in bondage because you thought that by being hushed, you were being respectful? Who's waiting in limbo for their breakthrough while you get the courage to do your part? It's time to rise to a greater level of boldness and not be concerned about the opinions of others. A sister's way out of bondage might come through your boldness to share the goodness of God.

Prayer:

Father, I pray for the boldness and courage to magnify Your name in the presence of others. May I never be ashamed of the gospel of Christ, knowing that it is the power of God unto deliverance (Romans 1:16). I come against any selfishness, insecurity, or doubt that may try to hinder me from sharing Your praise with others. Today, if there is a sister in my life waiting on me, I pray that she no longer has to wait. I will boldly do my part as You lead me to do so. I will share words of encouragement and love so that she will not remain in bondage another day of her life. In Jesus' name I pray, Amen!

The Extra Step: Today, make an effort to share the goodness of God with another sister. Let her hear you praise your God!

Never Stop Pouring

*"The wife of a man from the company of the prophets
cried out to Elisha, 'Your servant my husband is
dead, and you know that he revered the LORD. But
now his creditor is coming to take my two boys as his
slaves.' Elisha replied to her, 'How can I help you? Tell
me, what do you have in your house?' 'Your servant
has NOTHING there at all,' she said, 'except a small
jar of olive oil.' Elisha said, 'Go around and ask all
your neighbors for empty jars. Don't ask for just a
few.' … She left him and shut the door behind her and
her sons. They brought the jars to her and she kept
pouring. When all the jars were full, she said to her
son, 'Bring me another one.' But he replied, 'There
is not a jar left.' Then the oil stopped flowing"*
(2 Kings 4:1-3, 5-6, NIV, emphasis added).

wonder how many nights this woman stayed up worry-
ing about her situation. How many times did she pace
back and forth ignoring that little jar of oil sitting on
her counter? She referred to the jar as "nothing." I wonder

how many times we have done the same thing—failed to see that the answer to our problem was lying right inside of our homes or right inside of our very hearts. How often have we referred to our gifts, talents, and abilities as "nothing" or how many times have we mistakenly thought, *"I have my own problems, how can I be of help to you?"* No matter what your situation is today and no matter how much of yourself you have poured out into the lives of others, there will always be more to give. There was oil to pour as long as there were vessels in need of filling. The oil didn't stop until the need stopped. As long as there is a need, there will always be provision.

God will use those who are willing to be used; know that it's His grace that equips you to pour out of yourself. It is Him doing the work in you. If you make yourself available, He will give you more oil of His anointing. He will provide you with the wisdom and resources to help you keep *HER* and those around you full. So the next time you're worried or doubt your purpose in this world, just start pouring.

Prayer:

Father, I thank You for the opportunity to be used by Your grace. I thank You for the strength to keep pouring. Even when I am weary, I will rely on You to help me fill up a sister with encouragement, laughter, provision, or prayer. Help me to always be mindful that it's not all about me and that as I am pouring out, You will always have someone available to pour into me. I thank You for keeping me topped off. In Jesus' name, Amen!

The Extra Step: Today's extra step is simple—**Get to pouring!**

DAY 26

SPREAD YOURSELF THIN

*"There is that scattereth, and yet increaseth;
and there is that withholdeth more than is
meet, but it tendeth to poverty. The liberal soul
shall be made fat: and he that watereth shall
be watered himself"* (**Proverbs 11:24-25**).

t's simple, the more you give, the more you get. If you want to increase, you must be willing to give to other people. You can't be afraid that offering up your support to others will subtract from you. *It tendeth to poverty.* Let's not forget about the woman from yesterday's challenge; her provision, the oil, only stopped when there weren't any more vessels to fill. As long as you are scattering love, time, resources, and prayers into the lives of others, there will always be the same available to you. God will never run out of what you are in need of. *"Be not deceived; God is not mocked: for whatsoever a [wo]man sow, that shall [s]he also reap" (Galatians 6:7).* The prayers you have prayed on behalf of others are water to the seeds planted in your life. So go ahead and spread yourself thin, knowing that the more you give, the more you get.

Prayer:

Father God, I pray for my heart and the hearts of my sisters, that we will not be afraid of spreading ourselves thin. I pray that we will not be fearful of losing time or scared of the possibility of lacking provision. Help us to realize that there is no depletion in You and that You will always, always have more than we could ever need. There's enough of You to go around for everyone. Therefore, we can spread Your blessing to others without hesitation. In Jesus' name, we declare it, Amen!

No Extra Step Today!

DAY
21

GIVE!

"GIVE, and it shall be GIVEN unto you; good measure, pressed down, and shaken togetHER, and running over, shall [wo]men GIVE into YOUR bosom. For with the same measure that ye mete withal it shall be measured to you again" (**Luke 6:38**, *emphasis added*)

I f you truly believed Jesus when He said, "Give, and it shall be given," Do you think you would hesitate for one second to give? The reason we are not quick to give is because we are not convinced that it will be given back. When we give, it appears that we are losing something, but in reality we are gaining. We give. We get. We will never be able to out-give God; so while you are praying hers, God has someone praying yours.

You will not be left out! It's okay to pray that her business or her ministry flourishes beyond her wildest dreams. It's okay to rejoice over her success and celebrate when she doesn't fail. You water your own garden as you do this for others. The fruit that you yield will be good measure, pressed down, shaken together, and running over back into your life.

God wants to keep us in the habit of dying to self in order to live more Christ-like. Love is not selfish, it's sacrificial. Love gives. For God so loved us, that He gave His one and only Son, so that we can have and enjoy life on earth and in eternity. So the question then becomes, how much of the love that is in you are you willing to give?

Prayer:

Dear Heavenly Father, thank You for the opportunity to GIVE myself over to the challenge to PrayHers, knowing that as I give You are taking care of mine. I continue to pray over her business, her finances, her marriage, her singleness, her children, her health, and all that concerns her. May she never get weary in doing what is right before You. Strengthen her with Your mighty power and love. I pray that as she gives there will be other women ready to give to her. In Jesus' name I pray Amen!

The Extra Step: Today I challenge you to give a financial (Yes, Financial!) seed to a sister. It doesn't matter how big or small, just make sure it's from the heart. Money seems to be an area we struggle with in terms of giving. Our fear of lack causes us to hold back, preventing money to be measured back to us in the way that God desires. Therefore, I challenge you to give! And then watch the return come back to you!

REMEMBER WHO IS WITH YOU IN YOUR STORM!

CONTRIBUTED BY TIMINA L. SMITH

"Then he [Jesus] got into the boat and his disciples followed him. Suddenly a furious storm came up on the lake, so that the waves swept over the boat. But Jesus was sleeping" (**Matthew 8:23-24** *NIV*).

was in a whirlwind of a storm! I thought my husband and I were about to separate, my finances were all jacked up, friends turned out to be foes, and the list went on and on. The winds in my life were high—raging and crashing against my boat! Yes, I was definitely in a storm. But, I wasn't alone in the storm; Jesus was in the boat with me.

Did you notice that while the storm was raging against Jesus and the disciples' boat that Jesus was resting? Hmmm, so does that mean that while I was going through my storm Jesus was resting? Yes, indeed! But He wasn't resting because He didn't care; He was resting because He wasn't worried. He didn't allow outward circumstances to take His mind off of His mission and neither should we. However, the disciples had a different experience. They were weak in faith and afraid of not getting out of the storm alive. Thankfully, the faith and strength of Jesus saved their lives.

We all handle the storms of life differently. What may be easy for you is difficult for her, and what's difficult for her is easy for you. There will be times when you are weak and she will be strong. That is the beauty of not being alone in the boat of life. The Jesus in you will remain calm and in faith, rebuking the storm through prayer for your fretting sister. God has plans to prosper us and not to harm us. He gives us hope and a future! (Jeremiah 29:11). Pray a sister out of her storm today.

Prayer:

Father, I pray for_____. I rebuke the winds and waves that are raging against her mind, emotions, relationships, and finances. Let the calmness that is in Your love resonate in her soul. Open her eyes, showing her that she is not alone. You have equipped her with an army of faithful, believing women who will not back down from a fight and are standing in agreement with Your power to speak to the storm, expecting it to cease from its intimidation. In Jesus' name I pray, Amen!

No Extra Step Today!

BEAUTIFUL IN EVERY WAY

CONTRIBUTED BY DR. STACY LEATHERWOOD-CANNON

t doesn't matter whether you're the girly-girl wearing the sparkling jewels and high-heeled shoes or the tomboy wearing jeans and fixing cars, there's something inside of every woman that wants to know, "Am I beautiful?" Well according to Genesis 1:26, you are. God said, "*Let us make [wo]man in our image, after our likeness.*" Imagine that! We were made in the image of God. Who or what can be more captivating than God? The sun can't even shine more beautiful than Him. So regardless of what you think you see when you look in the mirror, the reality is that your beauty outshines the brightness of the sun.

Although the media would have us to believe that our beauty is all outward, we can rest knowing that true beauty comes from a heart that has accepted Jesus Christ as Savior. When you accept Christ, you become more God-like. You think like Him, you act like Him, and you love like Him. This is what makes you beautiful. This is the kind of beauty we should be craving. The kind that gives you confidence in who you are so you don't feel like you have to measure up to the world's standards. There is nothing wrong with looking pretty on the outside, but to beautify your heart is priceless. Kindness, love, and patience ooze a beauty that the world can't compete with, making you beautiful in every way.

Prayer:

Dear Heavenly Father, I pray that as women we will begin to see ourselves beautiful in every way, from head-to-toe. Thank You for loving us enough by making us just like You. Help us to love ourselves, on the days when we feel pretty and on those days we don't. Help us to never lose sight of what's important, which is to have a heart that is pure and beautiful. In Jesus' name, Amen.

No Extra Step Today!

DAY
30

YOUR HARVEST IS WAITING!

W hen farmers go out into their fields to plant their seeds into the soil, they generally don't worry about the seeds after they have been planted into the ground. Farmers do what's required to make sure the conditions are right for their seed to produce, therefore, they don't fret because they can't see what's going on beneath the surface; they understand that the seed has already been pre-programmed to release once it has been sown.

> *"Night and day, whether he sleeps or gets up, the seed*
> *sprouts and grows, though he does not know how. All*
> *by itself the soil produces grain—first the stalk, then*
> *the head, then the full kernel in the head. As soon as*
> *the grain is ripe, he puts the sickle to it, because the*
> *harvest has come."*(**Mark 4:27-29** *NIV*).

You may not be a farmer, but there are some requirements to ensure you don't experience crop failure. You must maintain a pure heart that loves, honors, and trust God. You must take Him at His word. It doesn't matter what it looks like to your natural eye. It doesn't matter that you can't see the evidence of your seed while it is in the stages of growth. You must maintain an unwavering assurance that what God has promised He is able to perform (Roman 4:21). Every seed has been commanded by God to produce on your behalf. Any act of love constitutes a seed. Your faith is the water and sun that will determine whether or not you experience crop failure or harvest.

When you go to sleep tonight, sleep in faith, knowing that the seeds you have planted will be working overtime to produce a harvest of blessings just for you. For the past 29 days, you sowed seeds into the lives of other women and for that, a harvest is waiting on you. God is going to increase you mightily. We don't always know how God is working out the details; we just know that He is. Don't worry! God will produce. By faith your harvest is already here. You will partake!

Prayer:

Father, I thank You today for_____. First, I want to pray for her heart. I pray that it is pure and free from selfish motives. I pray that You will let her know if she has any barriers that will prevent her seeds from harvesting. Give her ears to hear what You are saying. Give her the courage to obey without delay. I pray that she doesn't lose faith in Your ability to bring forth her desires. Grant her the patience that she needs to fight off doubt and unbelief. May she stand unwavering and confident in Your love and ability to cause her seeds to produce a harvest. In Jesus' name I pray, Amen.

No Extra Step Today!

God Will Never Forget

"For God is not unrighteous to FORGET your work and LABOUR of LOVE, which ye have shewed toward his name, in that ye have ministered to the saints, and do minister" (**Hebrews 6:10**, *emphasis added*).

ongratulations! You did it! Hopefully the last 31 days have challenged your labor of love. God is faithful and He will NEVER forget what it took to overcome the challenge of stepping out of *YOURS* and into *HERS*. God is hovering over every seed you have ministered during this challenge and He is saying, "You did it for Me and I will do it for you. I will reward you." Today is all about you. Whatever you need from God, just ask Him. His ears are open to your prayer. You have direct access to the throne and you will not be turned away. This is the day that the Lord has made, you can rejoice and be glad in it (Psalms 118:24). I pray that as you go forward, you will continue the challenge of looking for prayHer opportunities. Continue to show forth the true love of Christ. Enter now into the JOY of the Lord!

My prayHer for you:

Dear Heavenly Father, I want to personally thank You for the woman who so graciously took on the tough challenge to PrayHers for 31 days. I believe that her participation in this challenge was a divine set-up. You orchestrated her steps so that You can position her to receive many blessings. She has sowed patiently into the lives of others and now it is her time to receive. I pray that as she approaches Your thrown, she will not be turned away and that You will grant the desires of her heart. I pray that as she moves forward in life, she will always reach back endeavoring *never to leave a sister behind*. In Your name, Jesus, let my sister bask in a pool of blessings. Fill her heart with joy and peace. Amen!

#prayingyoursalways

The Extra Step:

Challenge another sister to take the *PrayHers 31-Day Challenge*, because *In Hers is Yours*. God Bless!

Wait! Before you close the book, I want to challenge you yet some more. I know the title said it was 31 days, but it also said it was a challenge, which means you are about to be pushed. This is that last leg before crossing the finish line, the last set at the gym when you thought you couldn't push anymore. I challenge you to stick around for the encore. Those that are hungry for more are the ones who stick around for the encore. They are the ones who get to enjoy a little extra.

PrayHers (The Encore): Do You LOVE God?

Contributed by Stephanie L. Jones

"There were together Simon Peter, and Thomas called Didymus, and Nathanael of Cana in Galilee, and the sons of Zebedee, and two other of his disciples. Simon Peter saith unto them, I go a fishing. They say unto him, We also go with thee. They went forth, and entered into a ship immediately; and that night they caught nothing...So when they had dined, Jesus saith to Simon Peter, Simon, son of Jonas, lovest thou me more than these? He saith unto him, Yea, Lord; thou knowest that I love thee. He saith unto him, Feed my lambs. He saith to him again the second time,

Simon, son of Jonas, lovest thou me? He saith unto him, Yea, Lord; thou knowest that I love thee. He saith unto him, Feed my sheep. He saith unto him the third time, Simon, son of Jonas, lovest thou me? Peter was grieved because he said unto him the third time, Lovest thou me? And he said unto him, Lord, thou knowest all things; thou knowest that I love thee. Jesus saith unto him, Feed my sheep" (**John 21:2-3, 15-17**).

D o you love God? I'm sure you're emphatically saying, "Yes! Yes, I Love God."

Now, let me ask you this, would God agree with you? Would He emphatically declare your love for Him the way that you do? Before you answer, pause and think about it.

The Scripture tells us that Peter was grieved because three times Jesus asked him if he loved Him. In other words, Peter was hurt, sad, and offended by Jesus' repeated question. But Jesus wasn't trying to offend Peter; He loved him. What He was doing was proving a point to Peter. He was trying to get him to see how love operates. He wanted Peter to understand that if he really loved Him, then he would have been out preaching the gospel and not in a boat going fishing with his friends. He would have been out feeding God's sheep.

Your assignment may not be the same as Peter's. You may not be called to go out and preach the Gospel around the world, but God does expect you to do your part and feed His sheep. Through this PrayHers 31-Day Challenge,

Jesus is saying to you, "If you love Me, then feed my sheep." Feed her with love, care, and compassion. Feed her with kindness and respect. Feed her with words of encouragement and hope. And most importantly, feed her with prayers and the Word of God.

Do you LOVE God? Then feed His sheep.

Prayer:

Father, thank You for showing me how to express my love for You. I now understand that loving You, means loving her. I pray that You would daily reveal ways for me to show love toward her. I pray that You would put Your hand upon my lips and Your words in my mouth, so that when I speak to her she feels encouraged and saturated with love. And Lord, I pray that her heart would be filled with love for other people. People will know that she loves You, because of the way she loves them. People will know that she loves You, because she takes time to feed Your sheep. In Jesus' name I pray, Amen.

In the Words of Jesus, "It is finished." I love you and I'm praying for you my sister in Christ. Thank you for sticking around for the encore.

dedicate this book to my parents. Without them I wouldn't have been able to write this book. My father, John Lindsey Jr, who is probably smiling down from heaven with a big grin and a proud father look on his face. His tough love taught me how to go after my dreams and not give up on my goals. To my mother, Sharon Lindsey, you are a true example of unconditional love and support. I have watched you sow great love into the lives of others—whether they deserved it or not. You couldn't have taught me a better lesson than how to walk in love.

To my husband, Freddy Dean, for believing in the PrayHers vision. You hooked up with it from day one; and it made all the difference. To my daughter Destiny Dean, you amaze me! Watching you grow up has helped me to realize just how important it is for little girls to be taught early in life about their value and self-worth. I love you, but God loves you more.

To my sister and brother, Charnell Gibbs and John Lindsey III, I love you both, and I am glad that we have each other. Thanks for believing in me.

To my nieces, Raquel Gibbs, Kasia Jordan, Kayla Gibbs, and Raenah Lindsey, I pray that you will always walk in your God-given purpose and celebrate who you are. And to all the women in my family, you are the epitome of beauty and strength. I pray yours!

THANK YOU

Thank you, **Stephanie L. Jones**, SURVIVOR, SPEAK-ER, ADVOCATE, and AUTHOR of, 'THE ENEMY BETWEEN MY LEGS.' You were definitely a God-send. You exemplified what this challenge is all about. You far exceeded my expectations by combing through the manuscript with such detail and precision. You treated this project as if it was your own and for that I am very grateful. Also, thank you for writing the 'Bonus Day.' Thank you A.C. Nelson for your editing skills. You put the 'sprinkles' on top and made everything perfect. The little suggestions you made had a huge impact. Thank you, **Markina Brown**, for staying true to the sisterhood. You have been there each time I have called on you. Thank you for taking the time out of your demanding schedule to read through the manuscript. Your feedback made a big difference. Thank you, **Dr. Stacy Leatherwood-Cannon**, PHYSICIAN CHAMPION OF CHILDHOOD WELLNESS HENRY FORD HEALTH SYSTEMS AND FOUNDER OF HEALTHY START 101, for not only reading through the manuscript, but also writing Day 29. Thank you, **Timina L. Smith**, FOUNDER OF VICTORIOUS WOMEN AND ELITE OCCASSIONS, for writing Day 28. You are a great visionary with a fire and passion to see women live the victorious life! Thank you **Jade Jemison, Adranna Jones, Felicia Maxwell,** and **Lisa Richardson** for being the four women, I described in the introduction, as the ones who *jumped in the ring* with me. Thank you for not leaving your sister behind.

I want to say a very special THANK YOU to the women I call, *The Genesis* (**Sharisse Brookins, Monifa Brown, Sherri Hill, Jade Jemison, Stacy Leatherwood-Cannon, Lisa Richardson, Robin Spencer, Cheree Walker, and Alison Vaughn**. You will forever be near and dear to my heart. When you showed up to my house on that noon day, December 31, 2011, we had no idea PrayHers would be birthed. I will never forget that day. The love and openness that was shared was electrifying and life-changing. We shared our desires and then committed to pray one for another. I pray we never stop!

Thank you to everyone who has connected with the vision of PrayHers. Together we are better!